A Benjamin Blog
and his Inquisitive Dog
Investigation

Exploring
Coral Reefs

Anita Ganeri

Raintree is an imprint of Capstone Global Library Limited, a company incorporated in England and Wales having its registered office at 7 Pilgrim Street, London, EC4V 6LB – Registered company number: 6695582

www.raintreepublishers.co.uk
myorders@raintreepublishers.co.uk

Edited by Dan Nunn, Rebecca Rissman, and Helen Cox Cannons
Designed by Joanna Hinton-Malivoire
Original illustrations © Capstone Global Library Ltd
Illustrated by Sernur ISIK
Picture research by Mica Brancic
Originated by Capstone Global Library Ltd
Production by Helen McCreath
Printed and bound in China

ISBN 978 1 406 27108 9 (hardback)
17 16 15 14 13
10 9 8 7 6 5 4 3 2 1

ISBN 978 1 406 27115 7 (paperback)
18 17 16 15 14
10 9 8 7 6 5 4 3 2 1

British Library Cataloguing in Publication Data
A full catalogue record for this book is available from the British Library.

Acknowledgements
We would like to thank the following for permission to reproduce photographs: FLPA pp. 16 (Imagebroker), 18 (OceanPhoto); Getty Images p. 9 (Lonely Planet Images/James Lyon); Photoshot p. 24 (© NHPA/Michael Patrick O'Neill); Reuters p. 26 (© Ho New); Shutterstock pp 4 (© VVO); 5 (© Richard Whitcombe), 6 (© Tyler Fox), 7 (© Pinosub), 8 (© tororo reaction), 10 (© Rich Carey), 11 (© R Gombarik), 12 (© Brian Kinney), 13 (© Krzysztof Odziomek), 14 (© stephan kerkhofs), 15 (© Sergey Skleznev), 17 (© Rich Carey), 19 (© Brian Kinney), 20 (© James A Dawson), 21 (© Olga Khoroshunova), 22 (© Ingvars Birznieks), 23 (© Kristina Vackova), 25 (© tororo reaction), 27 (© tae208), 29 top (© Rich Carey), 29 bottom (© tae208).

Cover photograph of Vanua Levu Barrier Reef, Fiji, in the Pacific Ocean, reproduced with permission of Getty Images (Lonely Planet Images/Casey Mahaney).

We would like to thank Michael Bright for his invaluable help in the preparation of this book.

Every effort has been made to contact copyright holders of material reproduced in this book. Any omissions will be rectified in subsequent printings if notice is given to the publisher.

Some words are shown in bold, **like this.** You can find out what they mean by looking in the glossary.

Contents

Welcome to coral reefs!

Hello! My name's Benjamin Blog and this is Barko Polo, my **inquisitive** dog. (He's named after the ancient ace explorer **Marco Polo**.) We have just got back from our latest adventure – exploring **coral reefs** around the world. We put this book together from some of the blog posts we wrote on the way.

BARKO'S BLOG-TASTIC CORAL REEF FACTS

Coral reefs are the richest **habitats** in the sea. They are home to thousands of creatures, from clownfish and porcupine fish, to giant clams, sea cucumbers, and sharks.

Coral builders

Coral reefs are amazing places, and I couldn't wait to dive in. First, I wanted to find out how reefs are made. They are built by millions of tiny sea creatures, called coral **polyps**. The polyps grow hard cases around their bodies. When they die, the cases are left behind.

BARKO'S BLOG-TASTIC CORAL REEF FACTS

Coral polyps belong to the same family as sea anemones. Like sea anemones, polyps have stinging **tentacles**. They wave their tentacles in the water to catch tiny creatures to eat.

Ready, steady, grow

Posted by: Ben Blog | 11 July at 2.45 p.m.

Tropical coral reefs grow along the coast in tropical seas. They like warm, clean, shallow water – that's fine for me, too! Tiny plants, called **algae**, live inside some polyps' bodies and help the **polyps** to make their hard cases. The algae need plenty of sunlight to make their own food.

BARKO'S BLOG-TASTIC CORAL REEF FACTS

Atolls, like this one, are tiny **coral** islands. They start as reefs growing around volcanoes that poked up from the seabed. Slowly, the volcanoes sink, leaving the atolls behind.

Daisies, mushrooms, and brains

Posted by: Ben Blog | 18 August at 7.52 p.m.

I've reached the main part of the reef and counted ten types of **coral** already. There are loads of different sizes and shapes. There are corals that look like daisies, mushrooms, and deer antlers. This is brain coral. It can grow to 2 metres (6½ feet) across. Can you guess how it got its name?

BARKO'S BLOG-TASTIC CORAL REEF FACTS

When coral is alive, it's brightly coloured – pink, blue, purple, yellow, and green. Dead coral is chalky white.

Fabulous fish

Posted by: Ben Blog | 3 September at 11.25 a.m.

It's daytime on the reef, and there are fabulous fish everywhere. In fact, more types of fish make their home on **coral reefs** than anywhere else in the sea. I took this photo of a **shoal** of butterfly fish. Their bright colours help them to spot each other in the crowd.

BARKO'S BLOG-TASTIC CORAL REEF FACTS

The parrot fish gets its name from its sharp, beak-like teeth. Its beak is perfect for crunching on coral and scraping **algae** from the rocks to eat.

beak

Coral reefs are crowded places, so fish and other creatures take it in turns to feed. Some fish come out in the daytime. Others come out at night. In the day, these soldierfish hide in holes in the **coral**. At night, they use their large eyes to find food in the dark.

BARKO'S BLOG-TASTIC CORAL REEF FACTS

If a **predator** tries to attack a lionfish, it's in for a painful surprise. The lionfish's feathery fins are covered in poisonous spines that it jabs into its enemy. Ouch!

Night hunters

Posted by: Ben Blog | 16 October at 10.59 p.m.

Tonight we went on another night dive. This time, I was searching for sharks. Whitetip reef sharks are expert hunters. They can sniff out fish hiding in cracks in the **coral** and wriggle inside to get them out. They can also pick up tiny bleeps of electricity that fish give out when they swim.

BARKO'S BLOG-TASTIC CORAL REEF FACTS

A moray eel hides in its hole, with just its head poking out. Its mouth is lined with large, razor-sharp teeth for catching any passing fish, squid, and crabs.

Danger lurks around every corner on a **coral reef**. Some reef creatures have special ways of staying alive. Stonefish sit on the seabed. They look like weed-covered rocks. But they also have sharp spines on their backs for shooting deadly venom, or liquid poison, into their enemies.

sharp spine

BARKO'S BLOG-TASTIC CORAL REEF FACTS

Surgeonfish have two sharp, spike-like spines on either side of their tails. If a fish is attacked, its spines stick out and it swipes its tail from side to side.

Living together

Posted by: Ben Blog | 5 December at 12.36 p.m.

Back in the water, I'm watching a moray eel getting its teeth cleaned by tiny shrimps, called cleaner shrimps. The huge eel could easily eat the shrimps, but it stays quite still while they pick dead **scales**, fungus, and bits of leftover food from its skin and sharp teeth.

cleaner shrimp

BARKO'S BLOG-TASTIC CORAL REEF FACTS

A clownfish lives among the stinging **tentacles** of a sea anemone. This keeps it safe from enemies. The fish does not get stung because its body is covered in special slime.

Slugs and shells

Posted by: Ben Blog | 14 January at 1.24 p.m.

As I was heading back up to the boat, I spotted this super-sized shell. It's a giant clam, the biggest seashell in the world. It can measure more than 1 metre (3 feet) across and weigh more than 227 kilograms (500 pounds). The blue colour on its lips is caused by tiny **algae**.

BARKO'S BLOG-TASTIC CORAL REEF FACTS
On land, slugs are plain brown or black, but sea slugs, like this Spanish dancer, have brilliant colours, frills, and pointed **tentacles**. Their colours are a warning – they are poisonous!

Remarkable reef

The last stop on our trip was the Great Barrier Reef in Australia – the world's largest **coral reef**. It's home to thousands of astonishing animals, including 1,500 types of fish, 400 types of **coral**, 4,000 types of **molluscs**, and some rare **reptiles**, like this loggerhead turtle.

BARKO'S BLOG-TASTIC CORAL REEF FACTS

The Great Barrier Reef is more than 2,000 kilometres (1,250 miles) long. It's made up of thousands of smaller reefs and hundreds of tiny islands. It's so huge that it can be seen from outer space.

Coral catastrophe

Posted by: Ben Blog | 13 February at 8.15 a.m.

All over the world, **coral reefs** are in danger. They are being damaged by **pollution**, shell and coral collectors, and companies drilling for oil. Huge patches of coral are turning white and dying. This is called coral **bleaching**. It happens when the sea gets too salty or warm.

BARKO'S BLOG-TASTIC CORAL REEF FACTS

This odd-looking creature is a crown-of-thorns starfish. They have up to 20 arms and are covered in thick spines. They have eaten and killed enormous chunks of the Great Barrier Reef.

27

Remarkable coral reefs quiz

If you are planning your own **coral reef** expedition, you need to be prepared. Find out how much you know about remarkable reefs with our quick quiz.

1. Which creatures build coral reefs?
a) reef sharks
b) coral **polyps**
c) sea anemones

2. What colour is dead **coral**?
a) white
b) black
c) purple

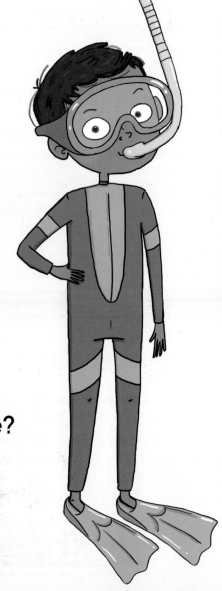

3. Which fish have two spines on their tails?
a) lionfish
b) butterfly fish
c) surgeonfish

4. Where does a clownfish live?
a) in a hole in the coral
b) in a sea anemone
c) in a giant clam

5. How big is a giant clam?
a) 1 metre across
b) 10 metres across
c) 100 metres across

6. Where is the world's biggest reef?
a) India
b) Australia
c) Egypt

7. What is this?

8. What is this?

Glossary

algae tiny plant-like living thing

bleaching turning white

coral rock-like material made by tiny sea creatures

coral reef long structure made from coral that grows along the coast

habitat place where animals and plants live

inquisitive interested in learning about the world

Marco Polo explorer who lived from about 1254 to 1324. He travelled from Italy to China.

mollusc animal, such as a slug, snail, clam, or mussel

pollution things that make a place dirty or damage it, such as litter, oil, and chemicals

polyp tiny sea creature that makes coral reefs

predator animal that hunts and kills other animals for food

reptile cold-blooded animal that has scaly skin and lays eggs on land. Reptiles include snakes and lizards.

scale tiny flap covering a fish's body

shoal large group of fish, swimming together

tentacle long, waving body part that some sea creatures use to catch food

tropical found in warm parts of the world

Find out more

Books

100 Things You Should Know about Extreme Earth, Belinda Gallagher (Miles Kelly, 2009)

Coral Reefs (Eye to Eye with Endangered Habitats), Precious McKenzie (Rourke Publishing, 2010)

Harsh Habitats (Extreme Nature), Anita Ganeri (Raintree, 2013)

Ocean Divers (Landform Adventurers), Anita Ganeri (Raintree, 2012)

Websites

environment.nationalgeographic.com/ environment/habitats
This National Geographic website covers a range of habitats.

www.bbc.co.uk/bitesize/ks2/science/living_ things/plant_animal_habitats/read/1
Learn about habitats on this BBC website.

Index